my itty-bitty bio

Jackie Kennedy

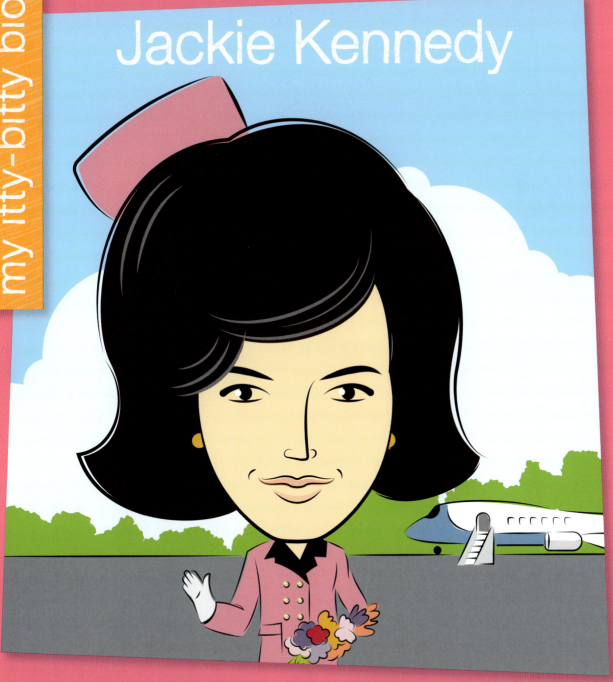

Published in the United States of America by Cherry Lake Publishing Group
Ann Arbor, Michigan
www.cherrylakepublishing.com

Reading Adviser: Marla Conn, MS Ed., Literacy specialist, Read-Ability, Inc.
Book Designer: Jennifer Wahi
Illustrator: Jeff Bane

Photo Credits: ©Americasroof/Wikimedia, 5; ©Public Domain/Photo by David Berne/Wikimedia, 7; ©Africa Studio/Shutterstock, 9; ©Toni Frissell [photographer]/Library of Congress/LOC Control no. 2015645223, 11, 22; ©Public Domain/Abbie Roe/White House Photographs, 13; ©Public Domain/Wikimedia, 15; ©Public Domain/White House/Wikimedia, 17; ©Robert Knudsen [photographer]/John F. Kennedy Presidential Library and Museum/NARA, 19, 23; ©David/flickr, 21; Jeff Bane, Cover, 1, 8, 12, 16

Copyright ©2021 by Cherry Lake Publishing Group
All rights reserved. No part of this book may be reproduced or utilized in any form or by any means without written permission from the publisher.

Cherry Lake Press is an imprint of Cherry Lake Publishing Group.

Library of Congress Cataloging-in-Publication Data

Names: Pincus, Meeg, author. | Bane, Jeff, 1957- illustrator.
Title: Jackie Kennedy / Meeg Pincus ; illustrated by Jeff Bane.
Description: Ann Arbor, Michigan : Cherry Lake Publishing, 2021. | Series: My itty-bitty bio | Includes index. | Audience: Grades K-1 | Summary: "The My Itty-Bitty Bio series are biographies for the earliest readers. This book examines the life of former First Lady Jacqueline Lee "Jackie" Kennedy Onassis in a simple, age-appropriate way that will help young readers develop word recognition and reading skills. Includes a table of contents, author biography, timeline, glossary, index, and other informative backmatter"-- Provided by publisher.
Identifiers: LCCN 2020035931 (print) | LCCN 2020035932 (ebook) | ISBN 9781534179974 (hardcover) | ISBN 9781534181687 (paperback) | ISBN 9781534180987 (pdf) | ISBN 9781534182691 (ebook)
Subjects: LCSH: Onassis, Jacqueline Kennedy, 1929-1994--Juvenile literature. | Presidents' spouses--United States--Biography--Juvenile literature.
Classification: LCC E843.K4 P56 2021 (print) | LCC E843.K4 (ebook) | DDC 973.922092 [B]--dc23
LC record available at https://lccn.loc.gov/2020035931
LC ebook record available at https://lccn.loc.gov/2020035932

Printed in the United States of America
Corporate Graphics

table of contents

My Story 4

Timeline. 22

Glossary 24

Index 24

About the author: Meeg Pincus has been a writer, editor, and educator for 25 years. She loves to write inspiring stories for kids about people, animals, and our planet. She lives near San Diego, California, where she enjoys the beach, reading, singing, and her family.

About the illustrator: Jeff Bane and his two business partners own a studio along the American River in Folsom, California, home of the 1849 Gold Rush. When Jeff's not sketching or illustrating for clients, he's either swimming or kayaking in the river to relax.

my story

I was born in New York. It was 1929. I grew up with brothers and sisters.

I loved to ride horses and read books. I learned to speak French and to dance. I also liked to write.

I studied history, writing, and art in college. I became a **reporter**.

What subjects do you like to study?

I married a young **congressman** named John F. Kennedy. He later became president of the United States. This meant I was the **First Lady**. We had three children.

I traveled the world. I brought art and **style** to the **White House**. I also became a fashion **icon**.

Then, my husband died.
The country shared my
deep sadness.

What do you do when you are sad?

My sadness didn't stop me.
I raised my children. I worked
as a book **editor** for 19 years.

I worked to **preserve** America's history. I helped make a museum and library. I saved important old buildings.

I died in 1994. But my life continues to **inspire** others. I paved the path for future first ladies. I was proud of my family. I was proud of the books and buildings I left for others.

What would you like to ask me?

timeline

1960

1920

↑
Born
1929

1975

2020

↑
Died
1994

glossary

congressman (KAHNG-ris-muhn) someone elected to serve as a lawmaker

editor (ED-ih-tur) someone who guides a book or piece of writing to be published

first lady (FURST LAY-dee) the wife of the president of the United States

icon (EYE-kahn) a person people look up to

inspire (in-SPIRE) to fill with a feeling or an idea

preserve (prih-ZURV) to protect something so it stays in its original state

reporter (rih-POR-tur) someone who gathers, writes, and shares the news

style (STILE) a lovely, pleasing look

White House (WITE HOUS) the home of the U.S. president and his or her family in Washington, D.C.

index

art, 8, 12

books, 6, 16, 20
buildings, 18, 20

fashion, 12
First Lady, 10, 20
French, 6

John F. Kennedy, 10

New York, 4

reporter, 8

sister, 4
study, 8, 9

write, 6, 8